A Life with Purpose

The Power of God Displayed Through The Struggles of My Life

by Kevin Berg

A Life with Purpose

This title is available in both traditional print and eBook formats.
Visit www.KissLimitsGoodbye.org for more information on Kevin Berg's speaking engagements or www.KevinBergBooks.com for information on his books.

Requests for information should be sent to:
Kevin Berg
126 SW 148th St., Ste. C100-449
Burien, WA 98166

ISBN 1-4116-2252-9

Printed in the United States of America

This book is dedicated to my family—immediate, extended, and Christian.
Your support and encouragement made me who I am today, a person who strives to seek Christ in everything he does. I continue to seek His face in my life because of your love.

I give special thanks to my wife, Melinda, for supporting me in my writing and understanding my late hours of work. I love you more than you'll ever understand.

CONTENTS

And we know that in all things God works for the good of those who love Him, who have been called according to His purpose.

Romans 8:28

(New International Version)

Chapter 1: Introduction

God has an incredible plan for you! I know you have heard this statement many times before—some might even call it cliché—just as I am sure you have questioned the truth of it. After all, we humans have so many imperfections that we look like meaningless little ants in comparison to an almighty, perfect God. This view is the main reason many non-believers will not turn their lives over to Him. They don't think they are good enough. In truth, no one is worthy enough to become a child of the Most High. Thankfully, He provided a Savior who makes salvation possible for everyone, despite all of our flaws and challenges. Christ covers those who believe in Him so that they appear holy and blameless in the eyes of the Father. In fact, God often uses our obstacles, weaknesses, and even our mistakes for His glory.

Christians sometimes forget that the Lord never leaves us. The New Testament writer, James, encourages us to be full of joy while we endure trials. This is probably one of the most difficult principles for a believer, new or spiritually mature, to put into practice. How are we supposed to be joyful when God appears to distance Himself from us? The answer rests in the reality that God's faithful servant, Joseph, knew to be true. The Lord is able to take our trials, the situations and events that Satan plans for evil, and use them in seemingly miraculous ways. Our Father allows us to endure pain, heartache and hard times so He may demonstrate His otherwise indescribable power in our lives.

Until I am with Him in Heaven, I will not know if God created me with a disability on purpose or if He allowed Satan to cause it to happen. The answer actually does not matter. God has used my situation to do incredible things in the past and continues to turn my condition into a blessing each and every day. You can see the gentle hand of God in various events throughout my life. I often look back on recent occurrences and piece together God's purposes for allowing each experience to take place. God's plan for my life is so specific that any change to any given event, no matter how trivial, would impact the final outcome of that plan.

As you read this book, you will see God's fingerprints on incidents that seem to have happened by chance and on trials designed by Satan to destroy my spirit and faith. I hope you will be encouraged as you read about my life, my struggles, my challenges, and the blessings that God formed out of each. I pray that God strengthens your faith, no matter where you are in your walk with Him, as you read about the miracles that I have seen God perform in the midst of my trials. I explain many events in great detail in order to reveal God's handiwork later. May you experience true joy by opening your eyes to the awesome power that God displays in your everyday life. Then you will genuinely understand and experience what Christ meant by having life abundantly.

John 10:10b
"...I came that they may have life, and have it abundantly."
(New American Standard - Updated Edition)

Chapter 2:
The Beginning Years

My Birth

My parents, Don and Charlotte Berg, already had a four-year-old daughter, Rhonda, when they learned they were expecting me. I don't think my parents planned on having another child, so I surprised them a bit. Little did they realize that there would be many more surprises to come...some bad, many good. My mom's pregnancy with me progressed fairly routinely, until she was involved in a minor bicycle accident. After that, the doctors kept close watch to make sure I experienced no head trauma from the accident. Ironically, the accident did no significant damage to me as far as anyone knows.

On the evening of March 18, 1974, my mother started having contractions and going into labor with me. My dad was home and able to help her get everything organized. My due date had been the previous day, but as my parents would later realize, I prefer doing things my own way.

Once at the hospital, the staff admitted my mom and placed her in a hospital room where she would be in labor and anticipate my birth. My mother's general practitioner, Dr. Nixon, came in to check on her and noticed some irregularities that he requested the OB/GYN check out. After he left the room, no one checked on my mom for a few hours. She was concerned because the OB/GYN never came to see her, and no one could find Dr. Nixon either. Early in the morning of March 19, a nurse came in and decided it was time to deliver. She paged Dr. Nixon, and he finally arrived in the delivery room after the nurses had begun delivery. Life, as my parents knew it, would change forever at this time.

I had apparently decided to be difficult and presented in the feet-first or Breech position at birth. Dr. Nixon, furious that the OB/GYN never checked on my mom, and probably mad at himself for taking a nap, began aggressively trying to deliver me. He was shouting orders to the nurses and pulling on one of my legs that was sticking out. Unfortunately, my other leg was still lodged inside my mother. As they tried to deliver me, more complications occurred.

I was born with a kink in my umbilical cord, cutting off my oxygen supply. My entire body was a dark blue, almost purple color, because I was not breathing. I did not take my first breath for over twenty minutes, and I was actually clinically dead for part of that time. God had other plans for me, though, so He allowed the medical team to revive me using mouth-to-mouth resuscitation, which certainly improved my day!

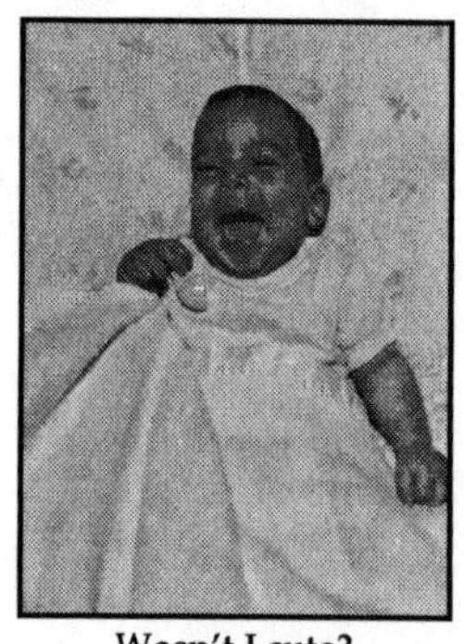

Wasn't I cute?

The entire time this was happening, though, my mother lay on the delivery table not knowing what was taking place. She only knew that they had rushed me over to a table, after I had come out, and gave me immediate medical attention. My father, on the other hand, knew even less. This was in a time when hospitals were very strict and did not allow fathers in the delivery room. For two hours, the doctors would simply say that there had been "complications" during my birth. I stayed at the hospital for about ten days because the doctors wanted to eliminate the seizures I was experiencing, before releasing me. Finally, my parents were able to take me home.

My Diagnosis

For the first six months, my parents raised me just like any other baby, not knowing for sure if anything was wrong. My mom did notice that I acted fussier than some babies did, but she assumed that was just my personality. When I became really agitated, I would keep crying and screaming. My mom would hold my tight against her chest and rock me for twenty or more minutes until I fell asleep.

After I turned six months old, she started noticing signs in me that bothered her such as rigidity in my limbs and joints. The doctors kept telling her not to worry because I would grow out of it.

Until I was approximately a year old, the doctors kept telling my worried parents that there was nothing wrong with me, despite the problems that occurred during delivery. However, my mom knew something was not quite right, because I was somewhat spastic. I was also not developing skills, such as grabbing, at the rate most newborns acquire such abilities. Finally, the doctors admitted that the lack of oxygen to my brain during my birth caused damage to it, creating a condition called Cerebral Palsy.

About Cerebral Palsy

The three most common types of Cerebral Palsy (C.P.) are spastic, athetoid, and ataxic. Spasticity occurs in around sixty percent of individuals with C.P. Symptoms include reduced movement due to stiff or permanently contracted muscles due to damage to the nerve fibers in the brain that carry messages for voluntary muscle control. Around one-fifth of people with C.P. have the athetoid type, characterized by uncontrolled movements caused by damage to the brain nerve fibers responsible for the inhibition of muscle control. The ataxic type, the third basic form of this condition, is unusual and generally occurs in just one percent of cases. People with ataxic C.P. have difficulty with coordination while walking and moving their upper limbs due to damage of the cerebellum, the area of the brain that maintains balance and precision of body movements.[1]

Some individuals also have symptoms that may fall into two or all three types of Cerebral Palsy, creating a mixed type of the condition. My parents would later learn that the motor-control area of my brain was damaged, creating athetoid Cerebral Palsy with some spasticity. Further tests would reveal that my brain had a higher percent of damage on the left side making the right side of my body more difficult to control.

I like to think of C.P. in terms of television signals. When you watch a station that is operating smoothly, the picture and sound on your T.V. set should be relatively clear and free from interference. Imagine, though, that damage occurs to the signal tower at the station. Inside the station's building, the show appears completely fine on the monitors. When the show passes through the damaged tower, however, the signal becomes garbled and static appears on your T.V. You can decipher the overall gist of the show, but the added snow is annoying. My brain and body work in much a similar fashion.

In my mind, I know exactly what I want my body to do. The message is as clear in my mind as it would appear in anyone else's mind. When the message passes through the damaged portion of my brain that controls my muscles, the

---

[1] "Cerebral Palsy," Microsoft Encarta Reference Library 2003. 2002

brain signal becomes garbled and its destination receives an unclear message. That means my body will carry out the overall action with added movement as well. When I try to move only one finger, for example, I move two or three instead. As a result, I require assistance to perform even simple, everyday tasks such as getting dressed, going to the bathroom, and eating.

The Prognosis

As my condition became clearer to the doctors, they painted a very bleak and hopeless picture of my future for my parents. They heard many disheartening predictions about my life—I would never be able to walk, talk, control an electric wheelchair or be smart enough to go to a "regular" school. The doctors made suggestions to my parents regarding the availability of special places for children like me in order to take the burden off the family. They were referring to institutions for people with disabilities where nurses supposedly took care of the patients. My parents knew, though, that many of the people placed in institutions at that time died at very young ages because of the poor conditions. Besides, my mother and father were already determined to prove the doctors wrong by making sure they gave me every opportunity to succeed. Although they were not yet Christians, I believe that God employed the Holy Spirit to stir their hearts so they would develop a passion for my well-being and my success. That fervor would one day lead our family to the ultimate success, a relationship with Christ.

Initial Treatment

Shortly after my medical diagnosis, my parents enrolled me in preschool and physical therapy at a place called *Children's Clinic and Preschool*. I attended there for a few hours a day, two to three days each week, to be with other children like myself and participate in a physical therapy program. While I enjoyed being around the other kids, the therapy program the clinic devised taught me virtually nothing useful and lacked any real challenge. The therapists had me doing simple tasks like rolling over, sitting up, picking up dowels from the floor and placing them in a box, and using a communication-board so I could point to pictures to communicate. Even at this young age, however, the Lord gave me an innate desire to develop my abilities, both physical and mental. I wanted people to challenge me more, and I actually wanted to use my voice to talk.

In various evaluations written during my couple of years at the clinic, the therapists always commented on my attitude, enthusiasm, and desire for challenge. One particular therapist, though, quickly pointed out, in an apparent negative manner, the fact that I was quite happy doing things my own way instead of the way adults instructed me. Little did she know that I would spend most of my life succeeding by doing most everything my way! I am sure that therapist would have been much more encouraging if she would have just instructed me to do exercises the way I wanted to perform them. I always accomplished the goals she wanted, so I didn't see the problem.

The head of the school, Dr. Holmes, acted even worse and put me on medication for seizures she claimed I was having. Fortunately, my mom took me off the medicine when she noticed it made me lethargic. My mother's decision certainly did not make Dr. Holmes happy, but she and my mom typically disagreed anyway. My parents knew that I had so many more capabilities than this clinic challenged me to achieve. The Spirit pushed them continually to keep searching for other answers and methods to help me unlock my full potential and realize the numerous abilities hidden deep within me.

Chapter 3: Patterning

The Doman-Delacato Therapy Technique

After many conflicts with the clinic's administration, my mom began reading *What To Do About Your Brain-Injured Child* by Glenn Doman. Fascinated by the development of the human brain, Dr. Doman and Dr. Carl Delacato created a controversial technique, consisting of very rigorous exercises, designed to help and treat brain-injured children. Believing that people can train the well areas of a child's brain to take over the functions of the damaged part, the Doman-Delacato technique centers around a single concept called *patterning*. Patterning relies on repetitive, purposeful movements of the child's body to teach the brain such tasks as breathing correctly and the cross-pattern of walking. God certainly created a complex organ when He designed the human brain. Mainstream science has barely even scratched the surface to the power of the brain, yet Doman and Delacato theorized this patterning concept nearly forty years before traditional experts.

The main therapy program using the Doman-Delacato technique demands a high level of commitment and time, and it adds an enormous amount of stress on families who decide to incorporate it into their lives. "Incorporate" is not even the correct term to use because the therapy actually *becomes* the family's life if done as prescribed. Parents receive training in this intense program by attending fifty hours of classes within one week, many taught by Glenn Doman himself, at *The Institutes for the Achievement of Human Potential* ("The Institutes") near Philadelphia. The family must then travel back to "The Institutes" every 3 to 6 months in order for the child to be reevaluated so that the program can be modified according to any changes in the child's development.

Since the 1950s, doctors and the mainstream scientific community has scoffed at and, in their opinion, discredited the Doman-Delacato therapy program. They claim to have performed case studies on the program and have determined that it is, in no way, worth the stress on the family. Possible neglect of other family members, physical and emotional stress, the dedication and involvement "The Institutes" demands of parents, as well as the requirement of 100% effort for success, are all objections these experts use to debunk the therapy. The idea they seem to portray is that parents should accept their child as-is and not desire any more from their offspring than what comes naturally. I have a very different opinion than the mainstream scientific community based on my experience.

"The Institutes"

After my mom finished reading Glenn Doman's book on treating brain-injured children, she immediately gave it to my dad to read. He read it within a couple of days and agreed whole-heartedly with my mom that they needed to look further into this therapy, which could become a possible breakthrough in my treatment. They proceeded to contact "The Institutes" and scheduled my first evaluation, which would include their initial training, for almost 14 months later. By the grace of God, our appointment moved to an earlier date due to cancellations, and we flew to "The Institutes" in mid-February of 1979, just a few weeks before my fifth birthday. Major changes in my condition, my abilities, and my life were just over the horizon.

Knowing that they could not do this alone, my parents, along with the help of friends and the local newspaper, recruited over 200 volunteers to assist in this home-therapy program. They would come in groups of three, once a week, for one hour. Eight groups of volunteers came in Sunday through Friday, and seven groups volunteered on Saturdays. Upon returning home from Philadelphia, we encountered a multitude of selfless individuals ready for action. Whether these people realized it or not, God had guided them into my life in order to change it radically.

During our first week at "The Institutes," we attended my evaluations and my parents had to go to lectures. Subsequent trips there consisted of the same basic itinerary. The experts there gave my mom and dad detailed guidelines, and they participated in hands-on demonstrations of the various physical and academic exercises that I would need to take part in several times a day, every day of the week. My parents received exact specifications of the equipment they would need to build and place in the downstairs of our house for my program.

In the mandatory lectures, "The Institutes" trained my parents in the philosophy that my success should be the absolute most important goal of their lives. The instructors even said that if I was in the middle of a therapy session and our house caught on fire, the session needed to be finished at the neighbor's house before calling the fire department. This program would be, in every sense of the word, strict.

"The Institutes" told my parents that either I would give them nothing at all or I would give more than my all and surpass almost all of their goals. The instructors there could not tell my mom and dad which route I would take. They did say, however, that my parents would know by the end of the first week, if not the first day. At the time, my two means of moving around the house were rolling over and scooting around on my back, both of which Dr. Doman prohibited. He established a goal of my being able to crawl on my stomach twenty feet by the end of my first week on the home-therapy program.

The Therapy

We returned from Philadelphia on Saturday, and my dad went to his brother's house on Sunday to build the equipment we would need the next day. Monday morning came around and I started my therapy at 8:00am. By 8:00pm that evening, I had met my goal for the week. My parents realized that I planned to give this therapy every ounce of my energy, so they called Philadelphia to find out what the next goal should be for the end of the week. I met the new goal within a couple more days.

Learning to crawl

I started out doing therapy 12-14 hours a day, 7 days per week. While my volunteers helped me with the physical therapy, my mom or dad provided the academic component with "flash cards" of pictures, words, numbers, diagrams, and other bits of information. I had some breaks throughout the day for meals and snacks, with one such snack break coinciding with my favorite cartoon, *Popeye* (I now have over 800 different *Popeye* items). My parents even planned the breaks with my therapy program in mind, with such requirements as taking several vitamins with every meal. I remember many days when I was so exhausted near bedtime that my body just wanted to quit before I was completely finished with my therapy for the day. My mind did not quit so easily most of the time, so along with the encouragement of my parents, I forced myself to endure the physical weariness and pain.

As the months progressed and I attended more evaluations, activities were added to my daily schedule that were certainly out of the ordinary, such as hanging upside-down by my feet from a hook in the ceiling and being spun around. Two utility workers were working on our upstairs deck once, and they looked in the window and saw me hanging upside-down in the downstairs portion of the house. They came running down the outside stairs and into the main therapy room because they thought I was being tortured. I actually found their reaction quite funny, considering they had mistaken my laughing for crying.

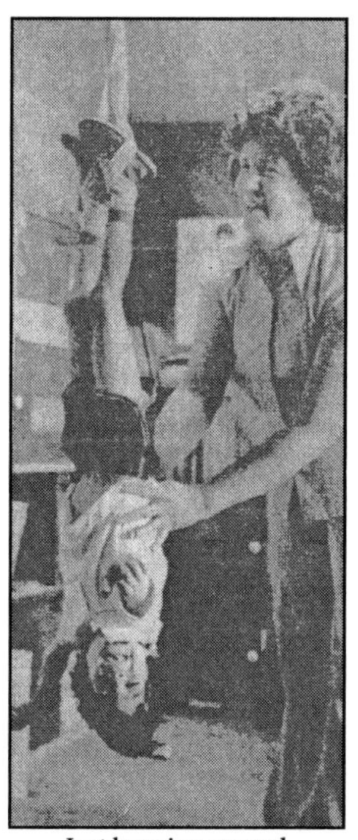

Just hanging around

Other therapy activities included putting peanut butter on the roof of my mouth to improve my speech, spinning around in a chair to help my balance, and masking to teach my brain to breathe correctly. Since most people with Cerebral Palsy have poor breathing, many die from pneumonia. Masking helps battle this problem. Masking consisted of wearing a plastic sandwich bag, with a short straw poked through the bottom, over my nose and mouth for a few minutes at a time. This meant I breathed in mostly my own carbon dioxide, with a little oxygen coming through the straw. An over-abundance of carbon dioxide in the body triggers the brain to make the lungs breathe deeper in an attempt to acquire oxygen. Over a period of time, the lungs become stronger and healthier. Carbon dioxide in the brain also helps increase brain cell activity, though some doctors would argue this idea.

After about one year on this therapy, I started creeping on my hands and knees around the house and soon learned to walk just on my knees. My parents decided, around that time, to cut my therapy schedule down to six days a week, taking Saturdays off for family time. Eventually, Sundays would follow suit, but we dared not tell "The Institutes" that we were not doing the program seven days per week anymore.

NACD

In 1981, my parents learned about an organization called the *National Academy for Child Development* (NACD) founded by Glenn Doman's nephew, Robert ("Bob") Doman. While "The Institutes" and NACD both claim there is no connection between the two, the latter program offers many of the same techniques, therapies and exercises as "The Institutes," causing me to use terms such as *the program* and *home-therapy* to refer to both interchangeably. The two main differences, though, are that the NACD program can be designed to be more flexible to accommodate a family's schedule and the evaluations are conducted more locally to those on the program. Once my parents helped organize enough families to participate in the Seattle area, Bob agreed to come out to this area for a few days every three months to lead the evaluation process.

Sometime during the first two times Bob Doman came to the area, a local television commentator, Ken Schram, decided to focus on the patterning program during one of his talk shows. He invited Bob to be on the show, as well as Dr. Holmes from *Children's Clinic and Preschool* to add the voice of opposition. Dr. Holmes commented on the "fact" that parents who pattern their children keep them locked in a dark basement with the shades closed and isolated from the world. Schram caught her off-guard when he asked my dad to come out on stage. After introducing him and explaining to the audience that I was on the program, he asked my dad, "Mr. Berg, I understand you and your family just returned from a vacation. May I ask where you went?" My dad replied that we had all just gone on a two-week trip to Hawaii, spending a week on Oahu and a week on Maui. Schram then made a sarcastic comment to Dr. Holmes about the fact that it sure sounded like my parents isolated me and cut me off from society. The audience chuckled.

Switching over to the NACD program would prove beneficial to the sanity of my family as well as the salvation of each one of us.

Chapter 4: Encountering Christ

We scheduled the first set of NACD evaluations to occur in November 1981, but we needed a facility in which to conduct the actual evaluations. Through contacts of a friend of our family, a local church volunteered the use of its building. NACD made arrangements so that our activities did not create a schedule conflict for any of the ministries or services of the church. The first time my father, who was not interested in religion at all, went to pick up the keys from the minister for a few days, he was surprised at the openness and trust the minister showed him. As the first round of evaluations took place and the second set rolled around the following February, my dad had the opportunity to meet some of the members of our host church, and their friendliness really impressed him.

In that year of 1982, Easter fell on April 11. My family typically attended church every other Easter, and I actually thought that churches only held services on that holiday. My mother grew up going to church but stopped after meeting my dad; he had technically been raised Catholic, though never becoming very active in the church. This particular year, they were trying to decide where to attend on Easter, and my mom suggested the church that hosted the NACD evaluations because the people there had seemed so nice whenever he talked to them. Easter morning came and we arrived at the church, with my parents and sister going to the regular service while I attended junior chapel. We all had a wonderful time, and my dad asked, as we drove away afterwards, if we wanted to go back the following Sunday. We all said we did, though I was just excited to find a church that was open every Sunday!

A little over a month later, we were all baptized, but I decided to be re-baptized in high school at camp because I forgot why I originally decided to get immersed. Summer church camp became an annual activity for me starting that initial year at church. In fact, my parents decided to purchase my first electric wheelchair to help me get around camp easier the second year.

Life in the Berg household changed quite a bit after we started attending church. My dad, a self-proclaimed alcoholic, quit drinking "cold-turkey" with the help and strength of our powerful God. My therapy decreased gradually to make more time for church activities. If someone had told my father earlier in life that he would be a church deacon, he would have laughed in their face. We should never put anything past God, though. He can take our lives and turn them upside-down if we let Him. He did so with my dad. My father became a deacon a few years after our family's baptism and served in that capacity until the end of 2001 when we all decided to find new church homes.

I can't really explain why, but I always had some kind of belief in God, even before anyone mentioned the idea to me. Common sense told me that things in this world did not and do not happen merely by chance, so a belief in a higher being seemed natural to me. Once I found a personal relationship with God and Jesus Christ, everything just seemed to make more sense to me, including one of the reasons that God allowed me to be disabled.

My disability caused my parents to discover the Doman-Delacato program. That program, in turn, introduced us to Bob Doman and NACD. As a result, we had to help find a place to hold the NACD evaluations and ended up locating a church that would act as the evaluation site. That church became the place we would encounter Christ for the first time. God brought us to salvation in that place. He built a spiritual foundation within our hearts when we turned our lives over to Him there, and we spent nearly the next 20 years learning about Him and growing closer to Him and His Son, Jesus Christ. My Cerebral Palsy acted as the catalyst through which God led us to church. If I were able-bodied, this series of events would not have happened, and my family might not be saved today. God's utilization of my disability in this incredible manner puts me in awe of His power and ability to take such a potentially negative condition and make it work for His Kingdom!

Chapter 5:
Expanding My Horizons

Learning Computers

Just about the time we started attending church, my parents bought me my first computer, a Commodore 64. That introduction to computers changed my life forever. A new world of programming, word processing, graphics, and games opened itself up to me on that wonderful machine. Of course, today we look back on the Commodore 64 with nostalgia because it was one of the very first home computers on the market. Today's computers have thousands times the processing power, speed, memory, and storage. The knowledge God gave man to create technology simply amazes me.

On this first computer and on the Commodore 128 that replaced it, I discovered that the best way for me to type was with my nose. That's right, I typed with my nose and became extremely good at it. My typing speed topped out at around 15 words-per-minute which is pretty impressive for pressing one key at a time, especially in that manner. A high school teacher introduced a different way of typing to me eight years later when I was sixteen.

Elementary School

Perhaps watching me trying to interact with other kids at church made my mother realize that I needed more contact with children my age. Because of this realization, she enrolled me part-time in public school at the age of ten. I had learned so much information through the academic portion of my patterning that I could have very easily gone straight into college! My parents, though, felt I needed more social interaction with children my own age, which was very true. I had spent much of my life, up to that point, with my adult volunteers.

When my mom informed the elementary school across the street from our house that I would be attending, the administration immediately started telling her about the fantastic special education program they offered there. Their assumption that I needed placement in a special education class offended my mom. Thus began her reputation with the school district as someone who knew her rights as a parent and my rights as a student. God had blessed her with a very stern, commanding presence and persuasive communication skills. In other words, the local school district learned very quickly not to cross my mom or disagree with her.

I can only assume that she explained to the principal and other administrators at the elementary school that I possessed college-level reading and math skills. She made it very clear that they would not put me in a special education class just because I was physically disabled. Once they realized that my mom knew the laws and her rights, the administration scrambled to figure out what to do with me. Finally, they came up with an answer.

I should have been placed in the fifth grade based on my age, but the school and my mom decided that I would go into a sixth grade classroom for two years because the teacher had a niece with Cerebral Palsy. The administration figured this teacher might work well with me. She definitely knew what to do with me, and she did not let me get away with much. I started out going to school just two half-days each week, and I progressed to two full-days and three half-days the next year. Ms. Jackson, who married and became Mrs. Gilbert the second year I was in her class, turned out to be my favorite teacher of all time. The newness of the school experience may have had something to do with that, but more than anything, I appreciated the never-ceasing challenges from this first teacher. She encouraged me by believing I could expand my abilities.

Class field trip

She included this one particular class activity, both years she taught me, which I remember quite well. She made all the students climb over the 8-foot wall that was in the school's playfield; two students sat atop the wall to help people over, if needed. Since this activity required a large amount of physical exertion, I assumed that I would be exempt from the requirement of scaling this barrier. I thought the woman had gone crazy when she informed me I was next! With the help of four classmates, plus the two perched on top of the wall, the class successfully lifted me up over the wall and gently lowered down the other side the first year. The second year, no one was waiting to lower me down on the other side, so I fell on to the mat resting on the ground, which didn't feel too good on my back, that's for sure.

Mrs. Gilbert encouraged my interest in becoming an author as well. In my actual sixth grade year, she signed me up to participate in the annual *Northwest Young Writers Conference* where I attended writing workshops for a day and students competed with each other by submitting stories they had written over the school year. I wrote a fictional short story entitled, *Peter and His Robot*, which told the amusing tale of a young boy whose home-built robot named Herbie is stolen by junkyard thieves. I based the main character, Peter, off of myself if I were able-bodied; I remember aspiring to build a robot when I was that young. The story didn't win any awards at the conference, but I sure enjoyed writing it.

I was constantly challenging Mrs. Gilbert as well. She would often need to find extra work for me to do in class to keep me busy because I finished the regular work so quickly. There were also times in which she asked me to allow other students to answer questions although I was eager to solve the problems. She tended to find it difficult to keep me occupied and to quench my thirst for knowledge. Near the end of my time with her, she recommended me for the honors program in middle school. I passed all the necessary tests with God's help and prepared to enter the seventh grade.

Middle School

My parents received notification that the seventh grade honors teachers wanted to meet with them a couple of weeks before the start of the school year. My handicap panicked the teachers because they had never had a student with an Individualized Education Plan (IEP) in their classes before. My IEP, written by my mom, outlined special services and accommodations that the school was responsible to provide for me, such as having an hour of therapy instead of P.E. and extended time for tests, if needed. This group of teachers, though, tended to equate IEP with special education. My mother agreed to meet with them, under the condition that they allow me to be present as well. Their concerns, as it turned out, stemmed from their lack of knowledge about physical disabilities.

They asked if I would be able to keep up with the schoolwork, and I relieved them with the revelation that most of my academic skills were college-level. Since my right arm tends to be more spastic than the left and does not stay down very easily, these men and women who were going to teach me during the upcoming school year asked how they would know if I was raising my hand to be called upon. In a tone that was probably more sarcastic than informative, I replied, "This is my left hand. If you see *it* go up, that means I'm raising my hand." Ironically, they responded with looks of enlightenment, as if I had taught them something they would have never thought of on their own.

I met approximately 25 of my peers the first day of the seventh grade–students with whom I would spend most of each school day for the next six years. Unlike standard-level classes, most of the same students attended all of the honors classes, one or two students varying by subject. I found this to be of great benefit to me. Hour after hour, day after day, from middle school through high school, I attended classes with the same core group of students who eventually all but forgot about my disability. Most of these students were more interested in academics than sports, which placed me on virtually the same playing field as them. I truly believe that God's gentle hand guided me into this type of class setting in order to maximize my social potential while minimizing the amount of teasing and ridicule I may have endured due to my disability.

During my first year of middle school, I left school one hour earlier than the rest of students every day so I could go home and participate in my home therapy routine all afternoon. I recall, quite vividly, my journey home that very first day of seventh grade. My family lived fairly close to the school, so I would walk to school with some friends I had met in the sixth grade and then come home from school on my own. (Note: I often use the term "walk" even though I actually drive around in my wheelchair because it sounds more natural.)

On my first day coming home, I didn't realize that relatively smooth path existed in the park I traveled through to make my route shorter. Consequently, I drove my chair through the middle of the park, over the grass, making for a very rough ride. I was cruising along just fine, despite the bumps, when I drove my front tires right into a deep hole! If that were not bad enough, my rear tires came about a foot off the ground, pitching my seat and my body forward about 25 degrees. I was more stuck than I had ever been before, especially considering my wheelchair used the rear wheels to drive. This caused the back tires to spin in the air when I moved the joystick, while trying to get out of the hole.

My situation worried me very much because the park was completely empty except for my cries for help. No one would be around for at least another hour when the school dismissed the other students, unless my mom and my assistant came looking for me when I didn't arrive home on time. Even if they had come looking for me, the park was rather large, so they would have had to search for a while to find me. My chair pitched forward so far that I could have very easily fallen completely forward at any moment, landing me on my head with a 200-pound wheelchair landing on top. To make things even worse, I really needed to use the bathroom, and the pressure of my wheelchair's seatbelt, especially sitting at that angle, did not make the situation any better. I finally snapped myself out of my terrified state and decided to do anything I could to get myself out of this predicament. I realized then that my feet, typically a few inches above the ground, sat on the grass in front of me. After saying a prayer and mustering up all the strength and adrenaline in my scrawny twelve-year-old body, I pushed with my legs and quickly tipped my chair back to where all four wheels were on the ground. I pulled the control in reverse as hard as I could to get my front wheels out of the hole. I quickly drove the rest of the way home, being careful not to hit any more holes, yet extremely proud of myself for working myself out of such a problem. My parents were quite surprised as well that I was able to achieve such a feat.

As I look back, I have no doubt that God acted on my behalf that day because I don't believe I could have done it on my own. The connotations of such an idea have a profound impact on our spiritual lives. When we find our lives stuck in a rut or caught in a vicious cycle of sin, God waits for us to call on Him for help. Then He provides the strength and the tools we need to get out of the situation. We must be willing at that juncture to take advantage of the solution God provides for us.

> **1 Corinthians 10:13**
> No temptation has seized you except what is common to man. And God is faithful; He will not let you be tempted beyond what you can bear. But when you are tempted, He will also provide a way out so that you can stand up under it.
> (New International Version)

By the eighth grade, I attended school full-time and did my therapy only part-time. I actually had to perform part of my therapy in one of my classes. During half of the two-hour honors social studies and language arts time, I would stand in a contraption called "Dutch Doors" which helped keep my knees straight while I stood in an upright position. I hated that time for the first few weeks because it was so difficult and painful to get into the device. It made me sick the first day and I had to go home early. Fortunately, I had taken classes from the teacher the year before, so she understood the situation.

This particular teacher, Mrs. Dominguez, was an extraordinary instructor. Having her both of our years in middle school thrilled all of the honor students, especially since she taught us for a period of two hours every day. She made learning fun while still maintaining a high-level of expectation for us, her students. We often reenacted various historical events such as the Nuremburg trials, and we even had to create newscasts set in colonial times, complete with commercials. Like other memorable teachers from my years in school, she constantly encouraged and challenged me to do better than my current best.

I enjoyed my time in middle school, meeting new friends and preparing for my time in high school. I started to learn quite a bit about myself and started questioning my priorities. By the end of my middle school career, the same teachers who were so worried about having me in their classes were saying that I taught them more than they taught me.

High School

As I entered high school, I found myself taking advantage of the ignorance of some of my teachers. They were very smart people, but many lacked knowledge about students with disabilities. I would tend to act like their stereotype or image of a student with a disability in order to get accommodations beyond those I actually needed. Granted, my actions did not portray a Christ-like behavior, but I was young and wanted to test my boundaries. Several of these instructors did finally catch on once they realized my true intelligence level, and then they would not let me get away with too much. One teacher whom I had for two years of journalism was the chief exception. He knew all along that I possessed more abilities than I even knew were in me.

Dr. Taeschner demanded respect from every student, even more so than other teachers did. Due to the fact that he had a doctorate degree, he gave detention to any student who slipped up and called him "Mr. Taeschner." He called all of his students by their last name in order to be intimidating. Many of my peers, even those who were not in any of his classes, feared him. In my sophomore year, I had Dr. Taeschner for honors English as well as journalism, and he definitely graded and critiqued assignments harshly. Sometimes, he literally sat in front of the class and read off the problems he found with everyone's homework.

One of Dr. Taeschner's favorite assignments included giving us articles to summarize in writing, and the summaries were to be "one half of one side of one page." He meant business and he was serious! One time when he collected our summaries, he cut them in half with a paper cutter and then read the names of the students who needed to rewrite their assignment in class because they were over the half-page limit. My summary exceeded the limit by just one line, so I had to rewrite mine! He didn't care that I had no computer in front of me to use, but rather he suggested that I instruct my aide to write small.

It is very true that many students disliked Dr. Taeschner, but he ended up becoming my favorite high school teacher. He returned the respect I showed him. He demonstrated his approval of a very few students in the way he talked to us, such as calling us by our first names rather than our last. One of the most important avenues he used in showing his respect to me was by believing in my abilities enough to encourage me to push my limits. While he was my teacher for journalism, he approached me and informed me he wanted me to find a way to take pictures. Hoping he would forget about this insane idea, I brushed it off by telling him I would look into it, having no real intention of doing so.

His sincerity on the matter revealed itself a few weeks later when my parents returned from the school's open house. My dad said that Dr. Taeschner suggested he help me adapt a camera so I could take photographs. A week or so later, I was taking pictures of our wrestling team in action. My efforts in expanding my abilities were rewarded, not just through receiving a district award for my photo-essay on Seattle's fountains, but by having the strictest teacher in school defend me to the end when a fellow student called that two-page spread a "waste of space." Dr. Taeschner always stood up for what he believed in, and it was obvious that he believed in my abilities and in me as a person. I left his class knowing that I had many more abilities within myself waiting to be discovered.

Dr. Taeschner's viewpoint of honor and respect can act as an earthly reminder of God's demand for obedience and reverence. When we obey and show God the adoration He deserves, He will demonstrate His devotion to us and those around us. The Bible tells of many people who prove this point. God saved Noah and his family from the flood because He saw Noah as a righteous man. Joseph became second-in-command over Egypt because he trusted and obeyed God through many years of turmoil. Daniel survived a den of lions because of his dedication to the Lord. Mary gave birth to the Savior of the world because she found favor in the eyes of God. Sometimes it helps to have physical examples of the various attributes of God. Dr. Taeschner served as my model of God's promise of support for respecting and honoring Him.

Early on in high school, my friend, Adam, introduced me to an entirely new level of computers. He built PC's and brought one over to compare it to my Commodore 128. The difference amazed me, and I convinced my parents to let Adam build one for me, which was actually more powerful than his. Ever since then, I have taught myself all about computers and software, becoming quite the expert in repairing, optimizing, and upgrading other people's systems.

In my sophomore year, a teacher observed me in the computer lab, typing with my nose. He thought it looked very uncomfortable, so he told me he had built a typing device for his neighbor that consisted of a stick worn on the head. I agreed to try it because he insisted on bringing it the next day. I had typed with my nose for nearly eight years and had grown very accustomed to it. For that reason, I really hesitated trying this device. I also did not want to use anything that made me feel disabled because I had grown up purposefully overlooking my disability. Doing this fostered a positive attitude and self-esteem within me.

For the next few days, I typed with this new device while in the computer lab, as to not offend the teacher who brought it, but I used my nose everywhere else. I found the "head-wand" very awkward to use at first, so it frustrated me to type with it. As I tried it more and more, it became easier to use. I started using it all the time and soon reached the point where I could type with it just as well as I could with my nose but with more comfort. Over the years, my dad constructed more "head-wands" as old ones broke or were lost. Today, when I am relaxed and on a roll, I can type in excess of 22 words-per-minute by typing just one key at a time. I typed this book this very way.

During that same year, Dr. Taeschner hosted a student teacher, Breanna Johnson, for a few months. She assigned the sophomore honors English students the task of writing a poem. We had to emulate the style of another poem, so I followed the style of Maya Angelo's *Phenomenal Woman* in my poem *Handicapable Kid*. Ms. Johnson thought that I wrote such an excellent poem that she read it in front of the class. Several publications have printed it over the years. I honestly don't understand why people see it as inspiring. I merely wrote from my experiences in meeting and interacting with new people. You can read it and judge for yourself.

Handicapable Kid

People stare when I go by
And I stare back.
They only know what they are able to see,
Not understanding the real me.
I'm a kid,
Handicapable,
Handicapable kid,
That's me.

Then they are put in a position
Where they must confront me.
The situation is awkward for them,
Sometimes awkward for me.
I'm a kid,
Handicapable,
Handicapable kid,
That's me.

We learn about each other
And they begin to understand,
That I only want to be accepted
Just as I am.
I'm a kid,
Handicapable,
Handicapable kid,
That's me.

They discover that I'm happy
Just the way I am.
Then they try to figure out
Why that might not be true for them.
I'm a kid,
Handicapable,
Handicapable kid,
That's me.

As I went into my third year of high school, I didn't dread the issue of college, as many students do. I had my life planned out long before this point. I would major in Computer Science at the University of Washington and live with my parents until shortly after I graduated. I planned to marry the girl of my dreams, whom I would meet in college, and we would live in a nice house, made affordable by my great programming job at the world's largest software company. Yes, my plan was infallible and nothing could change my mind...or so I thought. God, apparently, thought otherwise.

My sister, Rhonda, was my assistant for my last two years in high school. One day, early in my junior year, we decided to go to a college fair at the local community college. I went just to have a day off from school. After all, I knew where I would attend school after graduation. First, we went to the University of Washington presentation and I was totally excited by the end of it. We proceeded to the community college presentation because I considered attending there for two years before transferring to the U.W. Then, my sister made me go to the Seattle Pacific University informational meeting because she was considering applying to this private college. I didn't really want to go, but I humored Rhonda because I had already seen the two schools I was interested in attending. By the time the presentation ended, confusion had set into my mind.

Seattle Pacific offered features that attracted my attention such as small class sizes, Christian professors, and a more personal atmosphere. I was excited about the idea of attending freshmen college classes with approximately 30 students as opposed to a few hundred students per class at the University of Washington. Given my disability, the idea of more personal attention from the instructors very much appealed to me. Most of all, I saw the potential to nurture my Christian faith in a new way, especially considering that I had recently rededicated my life to Christ at summer camp. I decided to give the decision some thought and prayer.

In the months that followed, Seattle Pacific mailed me several letters and informational packets, while the U.W. didn't send anything. That was enough of a sign for me, so I applied to S.P.U. during my final year of high school. I received my acceptance packet about a month later. After taking all honors and advanced placement classes, I graduated from high school third in my class of approximately 230 students, with a grade point average of 3.89. I could hardly wait to start my college career! I had no clue, though, about the changes, trials, and blessings God had in store for me as a result of attending SPU.

Graduation Day

Chapter 6: My Life-Changing College Experience

I lived at home during my freshman year of college and figured that's how it would be through my entire college career. I had a couple of horrible assistants through my fall and winter quarters, and my college experience disappointed me because I was bored out of my mind. Both of the assistants I experienced trouble with were friends from high school.

The first one always woke up late, so I always arrived tardy to class. In addition, he wanted to leave as soon as my classes were over, so I never had a chance to meet any of the other students. The second aide simply had a terrible attitude and acted as a negative example in my life. He would actually talk back to my instructors and try to get girls in my classes to go out with him. Neither of which is appropriate for a student at a Christian university, let alone the assistant of a student.

To remedy my problem with assistance during classes, I finally hired an older friend, Bob Larson, for spring quarter, which made school much more enjoyable. Each day, Bob and I stayed on campus after my classes were over so I could meet other students and get a little more involved.

While helping me in the bathroom one day during spring break, my father encouraged me to get involved in some on-campus activities. He also offered to drive me a couple nights a week, but I couldn't think of any activities that interested me. Less than two minutes later, my phone rang. My dad answered it because I was occupied, and I heard him say "Uh huh, uh huh, great! I think he'll be there on Tuesday night!" The person on the other end was a student from school inviting me to visit a nursing home with a group of students. I went and had a fantastic time! I actually talked to other students outside of the school setting for the first time, and they invited to the weekly campus worship service on Wednesday nights. My new involvement caused me to become excited about school, finally!

Although I made some friends, I saw how well the other students knew each other because they all lived on campus. It made me long to live in the residence halls, but I thought it was impossible because of the amount of help I require. I jokingly commented to my dad about how cool it would be to live in a dorm with other students, and he told me that he had seriously been thinking the same thing. The following week, we met with the Director of Special Populations (after all, I *am* special!) who already had a plan in mind to make life in a dorm a reality for me. By the start of the next academic year, the school adapted a room for me in the dormitory called Hill Hall, and Bob became my roommate as he continued his pursuit of a four-year degree.

My dad & I did not tell my mom about my living on campus until a couple weeks before I was to move. We knew she would not take it well. When my dad finally told her, she feared it would not work out and believed I would move back home within a week. My dad responded by saying, "Maybe you're right, but we have to let him try." He actually knew I would be fine, but he had to humor her a bit.

Bob and I moved in to our dorm room on a Thursday, and it pleased my mom to see all the nice students who stopped by to introduce themselves, some even staying around to help. On Sunday, Bob and I went to church and then to my parents' house for the afternoon, even though I was anxious to get back to school. After we left, my mom told my dad that she had never seen me so happy. She was so right! An ironic situation took place the following summer, my mom couldn't wait for me to return to school and get out of the house, in a loving way, of course! Being away from campus life bored me beyond description, so I looked forward to returning to college life as well. Living in the dorms changed my life so much because it gave me freedom and taught me how to ask others for help. I didn't know at the time that other wonderful events would happen later in my life because of living on campus.

God certainly works in mysterious ways sometimes, even in events that seem so trivial. After a while, though, He reveals the mystery and leaves us in awe of the wonders of His plans. You can see His fingerprints all over each step of my journey to live on campus.

My sister played a major role in my newfound independence, just by making me go with her to a presentation about S.P.U. By hiring Bob, I connected with some students on a more personal level, which made me desire to become more involved in activities. My dad offered to help me get to campus when events were happening in which I wanted to participate. I certainly cannot describe what happened next as coincidence when a student called to invite me to a weekly activity less than two minutes after my conversation with my dad. As a result, I started taking part in other campus activities, thereby boosting my excitement for school and my desire to live on campus. With less than a week's notice, the school's administration developed a plan so I could move on campus, while the school approved a $13,000 budget for it the day after our meeting.

Too many events cooperated with each other for me even to consider that they happened by chance. God constructed this chain of events so I could live on campus, changing my life forever, as a part of His master plan for my time here on Earth. His utilization of something as simple as a phone call to impact my life amazes me and makes me extremely grateful that He knows exactly what He is doing. As I learned later, residing in a dorm would ultimately create other major changes in my life.

I declared my major in Computer Science during my sophomore year. The next year, though, I decided that I might want to do some motivational speaking down the road, so I added a Communication degree to my college ambitions. That meant being at SPU for five years and living in the dorms for four of those years. I had no complaints about that! Of course, I knew some students who were unable to finish one bachelor's degree in five years, so I consider my two degrees as a great blessing and achievement from the Father.

Even now, I look back on those years and a small part of me wishes I still lived in room 306 of Hill Hall. I have many fabulous memories of living there. During my first year in Hill, I unknowingly established myself as the resident computer expert. I once fixed a friend's computer in under five minutes after he spent four hours on the phone with the manufacturer's technical support with no progress. In following years, freshman would knock on my door, telling me someone suggested asking me to help fix his or her computer. Students in Hill Hall soon started calling me "The Computer Doctor." I always knew when someone needed help because the greeting I heard would be something like "Hey Doc!" I will say that it became a great way to meet the girls on the other side of the dorm!

I also recall sitting around in my room talking about life with a group of guys at 2:00am and all of us deciding to go to Denny's. Then, there was the time I found myself racing down the girls' hall at 11:59pm so I'd be out before midnight. I had been chatting with a friend for a couple hours, and then the girls at the end of the hall tried blocking me from leaving because they wanted cookies. Our floor had an agreement with the women's side that if someone remained on the opposite side after hours, that person had to make cookies. My mom looked at me curiously when I advised her not to ask questions if I ever asked her to bake three or four dozen chocolate chip cookies.

As I reflect on my time in the dorms, I realize I gained much of my independence during those years. Most importantly, though, I grew spiritually by leaps and bounds during my time at SPU.

Even though I had attended church for over ten years and involved myself regularly in church activities, I always felt there must be more to a relationship with Christ. The church my family and I attended taught us all about the characters of the Bible, the commandments God put in place for us, and the steps to salvation. However, the leadership never explained what it meant to have a personal relationship with Jesus and the impact such a friendship could have on our lives here on Earth. We never really learned about the loving aspect of God, only the vengeful side of Him. I knew in my heart, though, that Christ meant so much more to my life than my ticket into Heaven.

In the various worship and chapel opportunities at Seattle Pacific, I encountered a loving God. I experienced worship with people who were truly excited about their faith, a living faith that permeates every aspect of life. I learned that the joy I have in Christ is exactly what God had in mind for Christians in order that they may effectively witness to others. The contrast between the excitement I felt at school and the flatness I saw at church became so stark that I literally dreaded attending church on many Sundays. I feared the lifelessness there would drain the joy I built up over the week. Since my family attended that church, however, I stayed there and hoped I could help rejuvenate the congregation.

When I preached every couple months on a Sunday evening, I tried to show the members the excitement and passion believers should have for their Savior, but my words fell on mostly deaf ears. I suppose they wrote off my enthusiasm to the fact that I was a young college student. I didn't despair. I returned to college each Sunday night ready to recharge my spiritual batteries among peers who shared my zeal for Christ.

During my third year in Hill Hall, I acted as the Student Ministry Coordinator for the guys on my floor. I led the weekly Bible studies and planned activities that would encourage spiritual growth among the men. I always looked forward to meeting with the other ministry coordinators for the residence hall. We updated each other on the happenings of each floor, but we also shared in an intimate time of prayer and worship with just the eleven of us. I underwent much of my spiritual maturing during those times.

I may not have received the best grades in college as I had in previous schooling, but I graduated with a new sense of independence and a burning desire to serve Christ. My college career, save the first year, became the best stage of my life up to that point. It changed my outlook on life and on being a Christian. I committed myself to living a more purposeful Christian life because I wanted others to experience the power of Christ as vividly as I did. Unfortunately, I would watch that excitement fade away over the next few years.

Chapter 7: The Trials and Challenges of Love

Early Adulthood

After graduating from college in 1997, I kept my spiritual flame burning for a few months before the dullness of church slowly doused it. Between the lack of sincerity during worship, the many mind-numbing sermons, and various conflicts and deception among the leaders, my sister and I seriously considered finding another church to attend. We knew of several other churches with dynamic preaching and worship that we could attend to mature spiritually. In the end, we decided to persevere through the problems and attempt to do our part to improve things. After all, we basically grew up there and leaving would prove emotionally difficult. When the situations failed to improve, I really wanted to leave, but I relied on my family for transportation on Sundays, so I found myself trapped in a church that made me very unhappy.

In my personal and professional life, I experimented with different living and employment options. I tried running my own business building Web sites. The endeavor was less than successful because other people doing the same thing saturated the market. I moved between a couple of apartments and my parents' residence, for a little over a year. Finally, in September

1998, I bought my first house, which my sister shared with me until the beginning of 2003. An Internet-filtering company, N2H2, hired me in October of 1998, and I dissolved my own business shortly afterwards. I spent two-and-a-half years working on various projects for N2H2 such as a Web-based E-mail program and a search engine.

While I felt proud that people around the world used my programs, I knew there were pieces missing from my life. Computer programming did not satisfy the desire I felt to make a personal impact on people's lives. I strongly desired to help others change their attitude, their outlook on life. In addition, without a girlfriend in my life, I felt lonely and rejected. I grew accustomed to the same general response from women: "You're a great guy, Kevin, and someone will be very lucky to have you someday! I'm just not interested in you that way." Friends from college sent wedding invitations to me, making me wonder if I would ever find that special someone.

Meeting That "Someone"

In August 1999, God revisited the plan He had begun six years earlier when I started my four years of residency in Hill Hall. A friend of mine from SPU moved near me with his wife, Melinda. The three of us started going places together quite often. They became members of my church, which made me much more excited about going there because I finally had some close friends who really seemed to care about me. My involvement in church activities began taking on a new life.

I started becoming good friends with Melinda. She seemed so caring towards me, even asking me if I needed anything when she ran errands. I always made sure to tell her how grateful I was for the help. Over time, I noticed her husband treating her very poorly, yet, he didn't see anything wrong with his behavior. He literally took her for granted, never being polite or grateful. He even complained when she tried doing nice things for him that didn't meet his standards. I tried to point out ways that he could show her more respect, but he didn't see any reason to try to impress her since they were already married, and he refused to listen to anyone's advice. Seeing Melinda become more and more depressed, I did what I could to make up for his lack of consideration for her. I found myself in a difficult position.

On the one hand, I knew I was stepping over a relationship boundary. At the same time, I was helping a friend feel better about herself when she felt so unimportant because of her husband's disrespect.

By the next summer, their relationship had deteriorated to the point that I approached Melinda with the question of separation or divorce. She had been in a similar marriage several years previous and did not want this to end the same way, so she figured she would just live in misery the rest of her life. Any love that she and her husband had shared vanished long before this time.

I knew at this point that I had strong feelings for her, even though I knew she was married. Seeing her so miserable just tore me up inside, but I had no idea how to handle the situation. After all, I did not want to be the reason that their marriage ended. I admitted my feelings to a couple of people, including my sister, and they were sure that she felt the same way about me.

I had a miserable time as a counselor that summer at church camp. Melinda's husband went as a counselor as well, and we tended to avoid each other because of the conflicting ideas we had about marriage. He put on a front that made him seem like this great person, and most of the other people there thought he was just wonderful. I struggled, not only with that, but also with the fact that I had strong feelings for a married woman. I knew God did not approve of such things, but I also realized that He would not want me to abandon a troubled friend. I was thoroughly confused. After Melinda and my sister came to visit us at camp on Thursday, my Friday was wonderful because I had spent time with Melinda.

The night after we returned home, Melinda and I went to dinner together. We often ate dinner together as friends, sometimes even at the encouragement of her husband. As we sat in the restaurant this particular night, I struggled with the idea of telling her how I felt. I knew I had to discuss it with her, however, because I had the feeling she felt the same way about me. I also did not want things to progress further should she attempt to restore her marriage.

I believe that God allows people the freedom from a marriage if it took place under false pretenses. The man Melinda dated and agreed to marry became a completely different and abusive person after they wed. I wanted her to understand that, while she needed to try to work things out, she had other options waiting if everything else failed.

Talking to a woman about my feelings for her had never come easily to me, but this time the words seemed to flow from my mouth. I felt comfortable talking to Melinda about everything, even though I knew people at church would probably look down on me without being aware of the entire situation. In our conversation, she revealed that she had similar feelings for me. It was the best and worst night of my life. For the first time, here was a great woman who shared my feelings for her, but we could not pursue a relationship until she tried to reconcile her marriage one last time.

At the urging of a family friend, I decided to step out of Melinda's life so she could think for herself without any more interference from me. I knew I had caused enough confusion, and I could not influence her decision any further, in good conscious. The hardest time in my life began the day we cried together, after I told her of my plans to give her some space. I sunk into a depression like one I had never before experienced.

My work suffered severely because I just sat in my office and tried to keep my sobbing at a volume no one would hear. The thought that I had abandoned Melinda in her time of need rushed over me everyday. The fear she would forget about me held me prisoner for a couple of weeks.

Meanwhile, Melinda confronted her husband with many of the problems she saw in their relationship. He refused to listen or get marriage counseling, so she asked him to move out for a while. He called the marriage over at that point, but she didn't. She told him she just needed some time. Only a few weeks later, she discovered he had been trying to cheat on her for quite some time.

She and I had been communicating during part of this time, against the wishes of my family. Melinda felt abandoned by everyone and had thoughts of taking her own life. She is alive today mainly due to the encouragement I gave her in the midst of this terrible situation. The discovery of her husband's attempts at infidelity pushed Melinda to decide to file for divorce. Our relationship became public shortly after that, and new struggles began sprouting.

The Terrible, Horrible, No Good, Very Bad Week

In March 2001, my family and some of my friends tried to break up Melinda and me. My friends tried for three hours to convince me that Melinda was so horrible she would only devastate my life. I would discover later that, at the same time somewhere else, my parents were telling Melinda never to come near me again.

Those involved did not really believe that a woman could fall in love with me because of my disability. They would certainly deny that belief, but I still think it was at the core of their disapproval of the relationship. I had a large amount of money saved up at the time from a legal settlement with the doctor and hospital that delivered me, so my friends and family assumed Melinda wanted that money. They didn't understand the love we share for each other.

After the horrific confrontation I experienced, my friends tried to keep me hostage in the basement of my house by taking the phone off the hook while they talked upstairs. They never thought I would go out the door and drive my wheelchair up the hill to my aide's house. By calling her on my friend's abandoned cell phone, I knew that Melinda went there after my parents finished upsetting her. I even amazed myself by leaving, but I knew I had to if I wanted to be with her. While I was riding up the hill, I kept looking back, very afraid someone would notice I had left and come after me before I reached the house. I literally matured very much that day. As I drove up that hill, I recognized that I needed to start making my own decisions.

When I arrived a few minutes later, my aide and her husband rushed to get me out of my wheelchair and into their home. After a while, a couple of my friends came by to tell me how much I hurt them by not thinking longer about what they had said. I found it difficult to understand how they could accuse me of hurting them when they had caused damage to my heart that would take several years to stop hurting. They tried to make me leave with them, but I absolutely refused to go. A little while later, my parents came by and my mom started screaming at Melinda, calling her names. For the first time in my life, I shocked my mom by yelling at her never ever to talk to Melinda that way again. My parents realized that if I had to choose between them and Melinda, they wouldn't like my decision. They decided that they better try to get along with her.

Ironically, that day brought Melinda and me much closer. We knew that our relationship could withstand any trial because it survived the tests of that day. Although we still remember the dreadfulness of people trying to break us apart, we believe God allowed us to go through it in order to make our love even stronger and to remind us to trust Him no matter the circumstances.

The next day, these same friends and family members took me out to dinner for my birthday. Before we left for the restaurant, my so-called best friend, six years my junior, had the nerve to ask me if he could announce his engagement to his girlfriend at my birthday dinner, the day after he tried to split up my girlfriend and me. What was I going to say? I gave him permission to make the announcement since I was already depressed given the events of the previous day. I discovered later that even my father thought it was in poor taste for my friend to tell everyone at that time about the engagement.

Fortunately, over the next couple months, we discovered that the guy I thought was my best friend had told my family and other people many lies about Melinda. Discovering this made us understand my parents' reaction better, but it also helped my parents accept Melinda more. My dad even backed out of performing this person's wedding at the last minute, because of his lies and mistreatment of people.

Although the healing process from those couple of days may never be completely finished, I forgave all those involved soon after that fact, even though no one apologized. God says we must forgive others in order to receive forgiveness from Him. Doing so removes a barrier between the Father and us.

> **Mark 11:25**
> "And when you stand praying, if you hold anything against anyone, forgive him, so that your Father in heaven may forgive you your sins."
> (New International Version)

Besides, even though the pain of someone's actions may linger, being angry about it solves nothing. If I were to remain mad at those who wronged me, I would not be portraying the image of Christ to others. He forgave the people who nailed Him to the cross without them even seeking forgiveness. When we forgive others, we can release anger and frustration, freeing up energy for more constructive activities. In addition, we never know when more problems will come our way, so not letting aggravation build can make life much easier.

In hindsight, Melinda and I agree that we could have done certain things better and taken more time to develop our relationship. Melinda even realizes now that she had a part in the decline of her second marriage. Unfortunately, we cannot change the past. We can, however, learn from our mistakes, accept God's forgiveness and move forward. Clearly, even if Melinda could go back and change the past, her husband at the time did not intend to put any effort into the marriage.

Melinda and I know that we would have sooner or later been together. I truly believe that God meant for us to be together since the beginning, but Melinda had made some bad decisions along the way out of her God-given free will, such as marrying the wrong men. God worked through the mistake of her second marriage to introduce us to each other. I knew her husband because I had become friends with him while attending SPU and living on campus. Although Melinda went there as well, we barely knew each other. We really became friends a year after she married him and they started going to my church.

I know that God did not cause them to get married so I could eventually fall in love with Melinda. God does not ever contradict His values. I do believe, though, that He knew their marriage would fall apart. For that reason, He guided them in my direction so I could support Melinda through it all. Perhaps He allowed her to go through that relationship in order for her to realize how well I treated women in comparison to her husband. Whatever the reason, God continues to bless our relationship each and every day, even during the hard times.

Losing My Job

To make a hard week even worse, N2H2 laid me off three days after the constant attempts by others to separate Melinda and me. I could have been extremely depressed at this point, but I knew I had to improve my attitude for both my sanity and Melinda's sake. I decided to look on the positive side of things. They let other people go a few months before this round of lay-offs, so I must have been valuable enough to keep around a while longer. They didn't fire me which was my fear when my Internet connection was disconnected at home and I had an ominous message in my voicemail from my manager saying he needed to speak with me. My supervisors gave me high recommendations for future potential employers. God also blessed me over the next year-and-a-half as I sharpened my computer skills and hunted for a job. Standard unemployment insurance, for example, lasted 32 weeks with a possible 20-week extension for a total of 52 weeks. Thanks to a national extension due to the high unemployment rate, I received those payments for at least 70 weeks.

The Proposal

After a year-and-a-half of dating Melinda, I decided to take the plunge and ask her to marry me. On October 4, 2001, I proposed to her on her birthday. I had been planning the event for a few months and quickly altered the plans a week beforehand when she informed me that the school she was teaching at was having its open house that evening. As a teacher, she had to attend and meet students' parents. I had been planning on taking her to her favorite restaurant that night, but eating there takes at least two hours, not leaving us enough time to get back to the school. I quickly made reservations at a

In love

restaurant in a waterfront hotel, and the manager agreed to seat us before it actually opened for dinner so we would have plenty of time.

On the big day, our friend and housemate, Doug, drove Melinda and me downtown to the restaurant as his birthday present to her. He told us he was going to take a walk down the waterfront and come back to drive us home. I convinced Melinda to loan Doug her cell phone so we could let him know when we finished. We entered the restaurant, and the host seated us at a table next to the windows where we could watch the water and ships. A vase full of roses sat on the table, which Melinda thought was a very nice touch for her birthday.

After we ordered our food, I gave Melinda an extremely uncomfortable look. She knew that usually meant I needed to use the restroom in a hurry, so she asked if that was the problem. I told her that I just needed some medicine, which was in the van. She proceeded to pull some medication out of the backpack on my wheelchair, and I insisted that pills had expired. A little perturbed, she went out to the van to get the newer pills.

When she returned about five minutes later, all of the employees stopped whatever they were doing because they knew my plan. Melinda found me kneeling on the floor in front of her chair. She thought I fell out of my wheelchair until she came closer and saw that I had a blanket under me to pad my knees. We both started crying after she sat down, and I needed to ask her to marry me four or five times before she understood. When she said yes, I pulled a ring out from under the blanket and gave it to her.

When we both gained some composure, Melinda helped me back into my wheelchair and started putting my shoes back on my feet. I told her that I had more surprises in store for her, and she informed me I had done enough already. I motioned to her to turn around. When she did, she saw two of our best friends, Lynn and James standing there. I had flown in my previous aide and her husband from South Carolina because they had been very instrumental in the beginning of our relationship. Melinda nearly fell over when she saw them! When everyone seated themselves around the table, I revealed the secrets of my plan to Melinda.

Earlier that day, I went to the restaurant with Doug, Lynn, and James to figure out everything. Lynn even searched my backpack to take out any medicine that might be in there, but she apparently didn't look hard enough. I brought a dozen red roses with us and the host placed them on our table in a lovely vase before we arrived. From there, Lynn and James spent a couple of hours hanging out downtown and returned to the restaurant shortly before Melinda and I arrived. When we got there, the host told us that everything was ready for us, which actually meant that Lynn and James were hiding in the back banquet room. Every few minutes, a waiter went back to that room with something, from a pitcher of water to silverware, so he could update Lynn and James.

I panicked and had to think quickly when Melinda found the medicine in my bag. I felt like I took over a minute to come up with a way to get her out of the restaurant, but it was only a few seconds in reality. God must have been watching over me for Melinda to believe my poor excuse about the medicine being too old. While she went out to the van, Lynn came out of hiding long enough to help me get out of my chair onto the floor. Doug used Melinda's cell phone from a hideout across the street to call the speakerphone on my wheelchair. He told Lynn and me exactly what Melinda was doing so we knew how much time we had before she returned. He then took the bus home so all of us could go straight to Melinda's open house.

Aside from the medicine oversight, my proposal plan went off just the way I wanted and Melinda was very surprised!

Chapter 8:
Time for a Change

Out With the Old...

I seriously debated over the amount of detail I should write about leaving my first church. My family and I attended there for over 19 years, and I really do have some very good memories from much of that period. That said, I want you to know and understand that conflict, challenges, and pain can originate from anywhere, including the church. I will not use the names of certain people, out of respect. These events, though negative on the surface, helped to change my life for the better.

As the relationship between Melinda and me became more public, the atmosphere at church seemed to grow tenser. People had many questions about what happened to Melinda's marriage, but one of the elders asked us not to say anything. We even offered to go in front of the congregation, but he didn't see the need. As a result, rumors started circulating. About a year before I proposed, Melinda and I took a break from many of the activities we had been involved in so we could focus on straightening everything out with ourselves.

We thought the rumors had subsided and things had calmed down after our engagement announcement, so we asked my dad about the possibility of starting to get involved again. Since he met with the elders every week, he asked them their thoughts. He reported to us that they had no problem with us helping with the youth group or any other activity. On a Sunday in the middle of November, though, the minister asked to speak to us in a back room. He told us that there were still a lot of people hurt by what happened, and he wanted us to wait another year before serving in the church again.

Needless to say, that made us quite upset. We had already been through so much criticism and humiliation that we just wanted to regain some normalcy to our lives. My dad became furious when he heard what took place. He had seen much hypocrisy and deceit among the leaders in the past, and this was the last straw for him. If they were going to forbid members to serve because of what others thought or because of past problems, we all knew of reasons that each one of them should not serve.

Melinda and I requested a meeting with the elders for the following Sunday evening. At the time we made the appointment, we had not yet decided if we would be finding a new church or staying there. We prayed that God would make our decision easier, and He certainly came through. During that week, He revealed several more problems, including the fact that the minister was the one having problems with us and not "other people" as he told us. He also absolutely knew that Melinda and I had a physical affair before she even asked her husband to move out. He tried proving it by using E-mail messages he had received, and nothing could change his mind to see the truth. These, along with issues that had taken place over the last several years within the church, clinched my decision to find another church home. Melinda, as it turned out, was just waiting for me to make such a decision. We still planned to meet with the elders to let them know our reasons for withdrawing our membership.

On Sunday morning, God confirmed our decision. We spotted Melinda's ex-husband in a back room when we entered the church auditorium. We turned around and left. That afternoon, we met with my sister and Bob Larson, my friend and former roommate, because they agreed to go with us to our meeting with the elders. We listed all the issues we wanted to discuss and then headed for the church.

The meeting turned into a yelling match between the minister and me, while the other two elders just sat and watched. He accused us of all sorts of behavior that were completely false. He refused to answer my questions about why he had the right to serve when I knew several people that had problems with him. I grew so angry and distressed that Melinda and I left in the middle while Rhonda and Bob stayed to discuss other issues with these men. As we walked out the door, the minister made an extremely rude comment about my fiancé, and she literally had to drive my chair out the door because I wanted to run him over. I don't believe in violence to solve personal conflicts, so that should tell you how upset I felt. When we reached the parking lot, I burst into tears at the horrific ending to my nearly 20 years at this church.

My family decided to join us in our departure from that church, as did Bob and his family. My parents and sister stayed a month longer than Melinda and I because they were helping the children prepare for their Christmas program. They went to church each Sunday only for that purpose and left as soon as they finished. My dad didn't attend any more meetings, and left a letter in the elders' mailboxes resigning as deacon and withdrawing his and my mom's membership. You would think leaving a church after so much time and commitment would be difficult and sad, but we all actually felt a sense of relief and peace, as if we were confident this was God's plan.

...In With the New

A few days after our last Sunday at our old church, Melinda and I spent Thanksgiving in eastern Washington with my family and relatives. We normally would have come back to Seattle on Saturday so we could attend church on Sunday. Since we didn't know what churches we wanted to try, Melinda and I just relaxed and stayed an extra day. We really enjoyed our little break.

We went to a church the following Sunday, but it did not impress us very much. The worship service seemed more like a performance and the preacher spoke about health and wealth, saying that people who owned average or below average cars do not truly follow Christ.

The following Sunday, we attended Normandy Christian Church because I knew a family there who had left our former church. Since I actually told you the name of the church, you can probably gather that we liked it. We felt right at home and placed membership a few weeks later. Before we even decided to become members, they had informally given me the responsibility of developing and maintaining the church's Web site because they had heard that I did a great job.

The church leaders, even after finding out about why we left the other church, encouraged us to get involved right away. The fresh start at a new church set a new fire in my heart for serving God again. The people of Normandy serve the loving God that I discovered at S.P.U. and the sermons actually relate to our lives. I grew more spiritually in our first year there than in the last five or more years at our previous church.

Melinda and I were planning our wedding at this time as well. We had considered having our ceremony at a really nice and luxurious yacht club. However, we decided to hold the wedding at Normandy because of how beautifully decorated the church was for the holidays. It just felt much more like our style.

Chapter 9:
Starting a New Family and a New Life

Bringing Zachary into Our Lives

In June 2002, Melinda took custody of her five-year-old nephew, Zachary, because her brother and his wife discovered themselves in a situation where they could no longer care for him. At the time, the custody arrangement was only temporary, though we wanted it to become permanent sometime in the future. Melinda and Zachary moved into the extra bedroom in my house for financial and child-rearing reasons. Since Melinda and I were getting married, we knew we would be raising this child together. Fortunately, everyone at church totally understood the situation, and no one had a problem with Melinda and me living in the same house.

Many problems plagued Zachary when he came to live with us. He had not been to a doctor in over three years, so many of his immunization shots were overdue. His speech consisted of short phrases, no one ever taught him to ask politely for things, and his developmental skills were at the level of a two or three year old child.

In late 2004, Melinda's brother and sister-in-law agreed to give us permanent custody of Zachary which is a true blessing from the Lord because we had no idea if or when they would want him back. Zachary has just flourished while living with us. He has become a completely different kid. Although he does have some trouble forming sentences sometimes, he excels in many areas of academics, especially reading. He sometimes has trouble socially, not knowing the appropriate ways to interact with his peers, but he improves each and every day.

What a cute kid!

We believe he has some form of mild autism, but an exact diagnosis has not been determined. The doctors tell us he has "autistic tendencies," but they will not commit to a formal diagnosis. Still, he deserves and receives every chance from us to be successful. Given my past, I cannot imagine giving him anything less than the opportunity to better himself in every way possible.

Realizing My Passion

Typing away

As I neared completion of a yearlong programming course, I was awake at 5:00am on a summer morning trying to finish my final project in August of 2002. My search to correct errors in my code had kept me up the entire night, and I was still hours away from having a program that contained all the required features. Any excitement I had about programming left me several weeks or months before this particular morning.

A short time prior, a friend from church suggested that perhaps my purpose in life waited in something other than a career in computers. The idea took root in my mind and occupied my thoughts as I struggled with this project. I realized early that morning that I didn't want to have a career that would make me pull out my hair. Nor, did I want to have a job that consumed all my free time trying to keep up with new technologies and innovations in order to stay employable. Every job requires life-long improvement, it is true, but many people in the computer industry have little family or leisure time. Besides, my true passion waited for me elsewhere.

Throughout my life, encouraging others has come naturally to me. Often I inspire people without even saying anything, and other times I motivate people by telling them about my life and the attitude that has helped me overcome challenge after challenge. Touching people's lives has always been my one of my true passions. As I mentioned earlier, I received a college degree in Communication with the dream of using it as a speaker. Restrained by my physical abilities and unclear speech, though, I reserved myself to the idea that working with computers was the only profession realistic for me to pursue. Finding no happiness or reward in programming, I concluded that I didn't even want to do that. Ignoring everything I learned in my life about abilities, I discovered I had put limits on myself. The time had come for me to shed those mental obstacles and turn my dreams into reality.

Using my creative thinking, I approached Melinda with the idea of us speaking as a team, with her repeating everything I say, so people would be sure to understand. Seeing the passion in my eyes and the excitement in my voice, she actually stepped down from her teaching position in hopes that our speaking team, called *Keep Movin'*, was to become in high demand. Unfortunately, business started very slowly, so we had very little income for a couple of years. Sometimes, we considered giving up, but God would always get us back on the right path by either sending us some work the next day or allowing us to receive unexpected money. Two-and-a-half years later, our speaking services finally seem to be requested more often, but we have a long way to go before our schedule fills up. This is all right, however, because this seems to be exactly what God wants us to be doing.

He keeps showing us little signs telling us that we need to trust Him because He has something very special planned for us. I have no other choice but to put my faith in Him because He has never let me down.

Melinda and I absolutely love what we do, and every speaking event encourages us and serves as a reminder of our passion for people. We speak at schools and business across the United States, and we especially enjoy speaking at churches, encouraging believers to take full advantage of the joy the Lord has to offer. Second only to speaking is my passion for writing books of encouragement and inspiration. Melinda and I want to see Christians live the abundant life that Christ promised—a life full of joy, a life free from worry, and a life that acts as a witness for Him.

Getting Married

On December 21, 2002, I married the wonderful Melinda Jeanne Conley, the love of my life. My parents actually paid for a large portion of our wedding and honeymoon, a very positive sign that they accepted our relationship. Bob Larson wrote music for a poem I had written when Melinda and I first started dating. My loving sister and her friend sang it at the wedding while Bob played the piano. I started crying out of happiness and love as soon as I heard the beautiful music.

Surprise!

We surprised everyone at the end of the ceremony when Melinda stood me up to kiss her. We warned a few people in the wedding party ahead of time, just in case we needed help. As it turned out, Melinda had difficulty sitting me back down, so Lynn assisted me back into my chair. My mom said she had been able to hold back the tears until I stood!

Angel on Earth

God sent an angel from above
In the form of the one I love
That precious heavenly being is you
The one who makes me feel brand new

It seems that whenever you are near
My problems all just disappear
Worries vanish and leave no trace
A demonstration of our God's grace

On the day your face I first saw
God's masterpiece left me in awe
The sparkle in your eyes of blue
Shows me that this love is true

There is nothing in this world that can show
How my love for you daily grows
No words can express, no actions describe
The joy I feel deep down inside

You have brought a glimpse of Heaven to me
And the rest I can not wait to see
Until that time, at least I know
My angel will always love me so

My new wife and I spent two weeks in New York City during the holidays for our honeymoon. That vacation was the best either one of us has ever had in our lives so far! It snowed on Christmas day there for the first time in 30 years, so we took a carriage ride through Central Park in the falling snow on Christmas. The holidays don't get any more romantic than that!

Each year of our relationship improves on the previous. We support each other in everything, and we tackle problems side-by-side. We celebrate events in our lives no matter how big or small they seem to others. The most important event so far in our lives began on Valentine's Day 2004 when we found out that Melinda was expecting our first child. Although we consider Zachary to be our child, becoming parents to our biological child differs in many ways to becoming parents of someone else's child. Over the next few months, we learned we were expecting a girl and she would be born in the middle of October. Sometimes things don't go as expected.

The Miracle Named Gabriella

The previous June, Melinda's sister, Julie, gave birth to her son about 8 weeks early due to a potentially fatal condition in the mother called preeclampsia. Melinda's dad and Julie are both doctors, so they started giving Melinda the warning signs of preeclampsia as soon as we told them we were expecting and during the several months that followed. They said Melinda was at a higher risk due to family history. I tended to ignore them and figured they were just being overly paranoid because of the previous experience. Melinda ended up taking their advice with a grain of salt, partly because of my non-concern. A few months into her pregnancy, she started experiencing spikes in her blood pressure, but whenever a symptom like this would arise, we would not take it too seriously because no other symptoms accompanied it.

On Wednesday, July 22, we headed out to a three-day Christian musical festival at the Gorge in central Washington, about 150 miles from where we lived. We invited our friend and my former personal aide, Lynn, to join us. Lynn would help me with my needs because Melinda had just entered her third trimester and could not transfer me without risking the safety of the baby. Zachary had spent the night with Melinda's parents, so the three of us stopped to pick him up on the way out of town. As a precaution, my father-in-law measured Melinda's blood pressure and got a reading of 180/110, which is extremely high. We turned around and went to our local hospital where the maternity clinic monitored Melinda for a couple of hours and then released her. Her blood pressure had dropped to a safe level on the way and everything looked all right with the baby. We decided to leave for the Gorge the next morning, since the hospital had given Melinda permission to go still.

We arrived in the early afternoon the next day and set up camp. Melinda and Lynn were tired from putting up our tents, so we ate lunch and tried to relax in the scorching afternoon sun. After drinking our fair share of water and eating a quick dinner, we took the shuttle down to the main stage to enjoy the evening's bands. The Gorge's staff, unfortunately, forced me to sit in the designated wheelchair section, meaning that everyone with me either had to sit on the concrete or away from me. We listened to a few songs, and I could tell Melinda was uncomfortable sitting on the ground. At my suggestion, she and Lynn returned to camp to retrieve the camping chairs, while Zachary and I stayed to listen to the next group. I began to worry when the ladies had not returned by the end of the next set.

My favorite group was going to start playing soon, but I took Zachary to the shuttle pick-up location so we could go back to our campsite and find out what happened to the other two. In previous years, we had never waited for a shuttle more than 15 minutes, but this time Zachary and I waited for what seemed like an eternity. I heard the next band begin playing, and I let out a disappointed groan knowing I would miss the entire performance. The van arrived after nearly 30 minutes.

Lynn arrived as I was about to drive my chair on to the wheelchair lift. "We have a problem," she said, "they're going to take Melinda to the hospital." As we rode the shuttle to the first aid tent, Lynn updated me. Apparently, Melinda had wanted to stop and check her blood pressure on the way back to the main stage. The volunteer nurse that helped her had 28 years of obstetrics experience and showed much concern over Melinda's blood pressure reading of 165/110. As the nurse brought out an I.V., Melinda told Lynn to find me. I consider God's timing to be a huge blessing. If Zachary and I would have caught a shuttle any sooner, Lynn could have searched for over an hour before finding us.

Lynn, Zachary and I arrived just as the nurse was getting ready to give Melinda her first dose of magnesium to help lower her blood pressure. Magnesium, as the nurse warned, gives an intense warming sensation throughout the entire body. Sure enough, Melinda said she felt like she was on fire! The doctor on duty happened to be an obstetrician, and he recommended Melinda be transported via ambulance to the nearest hospital, 45 miles away. As I watched the ambulance pull away, I cried, not quite knowing what was happening and not being able to ride in the ambulance with my sweetheart. Another nurse came over and prayed with me as I waited for Lynn to bring our van around.

We found the hospital 20 minutes after Melinda arrived. They monitored her for a couple hours before deciding to airlift her to the University of Washington Medical Center in Seattle, a place we would become very familiar over the next few months. The rest of us drove back to the Gorge to gather our belongings, but we left our large tent and asked someone to place a "FREE" sign on it.

We left the Gorge at around 7:00am on Friday morning, eating sandwiches, which Lynn made while she packed. We took Melinda's cell phone so we could keep in contact with her parents and my sister, all of whom met her at the hospital until I could get there. My parents flew to Minnesota the day before to visit my grandma, so my sister called them. We arrived at the U.W. Medical Center around 10:00am, two hours after my wife.

The doctors diagnosed Melinda with preeclampsia, the only cure to which is delivering the baby. We estimated that she was about 28 weeks along, 12 weeks away from her due date. The team of doctors informed us that this hospital treated preeclampsia very aggressively, meaning that they try to keep the baby in the womb for as long as possible. They hoped Melinda could carry the baby for at least two more weeks. If they waited too long, though, Melinda's vital organs would begin shutting down, resulting in the loss of both mother and baby.

They stabilized Melinda through Sunday morning. That evening, the nurse informed Melinda that her latest blood tests concerned the doctors, and they requested that the nurse run further tests in a few hours. Five minutes later, a team of doctors walked into the hospital room. It is never a good sign when four doctors come into someone's room at 9:30pm. They told us that they needed to perform a C-section on Melinda or else she could go into a coma in the next 24 hours. Gabriella Jeanne Berg ("Gabbie" for short) was born at 11:18pm that evening, July 25, 2004, weighing just 1 pound and 14 ounces.

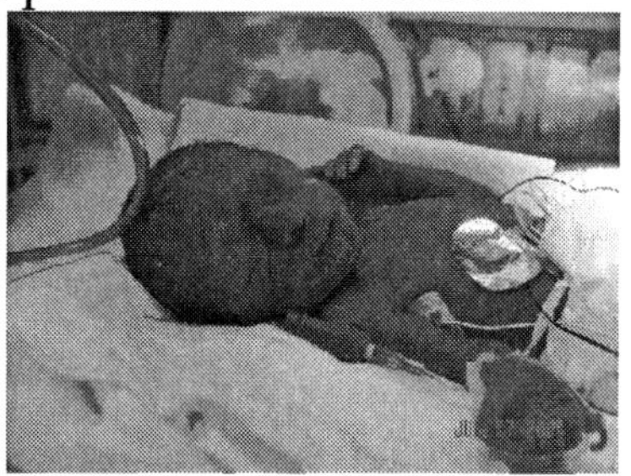

Gabriella Jeanne Berg at just 2 days old

My dad flew home the next day to be with us. Melinda remained hospitalized until the following Saturday. Gabbie spent 75 days in the neonatal intensive care unit (NICU), being released on October 8, six days before her original due date. She improved her health and grew rapidly, avoiding many of the complications most babies her size experience. Melinda and I visited her for a few hours every day, and a wonderful group of nurses took care of her. We faced two-and-a-half rough months of traveling back and forth to the hospital, sometimes twice a day. In the middle of all of this, we moved into the basement of my parents' house, my sister got married, and she moved into our old house with her new husband, Greg. It was an extremely busy and stressful summer to say the least.

God once again revealed the perfection of His plans that summer. He wanted us to go to that music festival. Melinda checked her blood pressure only because of the heat at the Gorge. If we had not been there, she probably would have waited a few more days to check her blood pressure and that would have been too late. We saw God at the first aid tent, as well, where He placed a nurse and a doctor experienced in pregnancies.

The Lord also watched over our financial situation. About a month before Gabbie was born, Melinda discovered that she qualified for state insurance, which would cover anything our primary insurance did not. The state insurance would cover her until two months after giving birth, and the baby would automatically receive coverage. Given the circumstances, our medical bills topped $200,000 with over $40,000 not covered by our primary insurance. As I said earlier, we were already struggling making ends meet. I found out that if we made just $700 a month more, the state would have denied Melinda the supplemental insurance, leaving us with over $40,000 to pay the hospital. As it stands now, we have not paid a single penny! God had a very good reason for us to struggle financially, and we feel a bit ashamed now for complaining at the time. We just needed another reminder that God allows us to go through trials sometimes so He can provide blessings.

Another goal God had by providing us with very little money was for us to move into the downstairs of my parents' house. We originally agreed to the arrangement for financial reasons, but Melinda would soon learn that she could not take care of Gabbie and help me out at the same time, so my parents have been a huge blessing. Moreover, Melinda and my mom have grown much closer, which I thought would never happen.

The release of Gabriella from the hospital excited and relieved our entire family, but Melinda and I were beside ourselves with joy as was Zachary, her "big brother." We kept her in the house for the first two months because premature babies have underdeveloped immune systems. By the start of the 2004 holiday season, we ventured out with her more and she loved looking at all the new sights, especially the Christmas lights at the mall! The local community newspaper even ran a Christmas article about our little miracle. As the year 2005 rolled around, Gabbie was gaining weight like crazy, putting on a pound every couple of weeks! She gets the most adorable expressions on her face. My heart melts each and every time she smiles at me…what an incredible feeling!

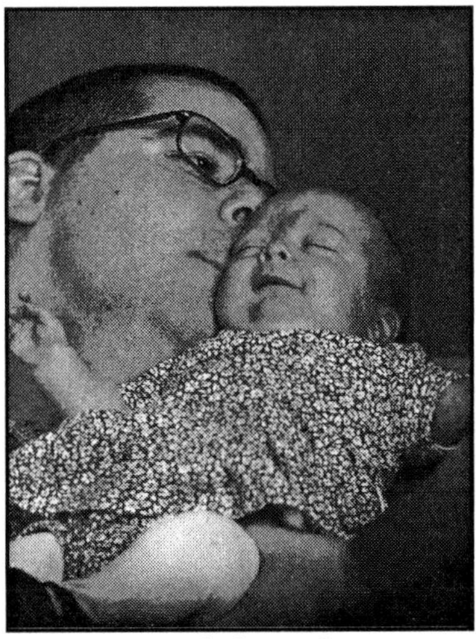

My little angel

My wife, our children, and I may not have much money right now, but I thank God everyday for all the blessings He bestows upon us. Gifts that seem small to some people mean the world to me! After all, we don't deserve *anything* from the Lord, yet He sees fit to take care of those who place their full trust in Him. I will raise my family in that faith and believing that salvation for those around us and ourselves is the only aspect of life that really matters. Everything of this world is temporary. Our physical life is but a blink of the eye compared to the incredible eternal life in Heaven that Christ offers each of us. I won't complain if God decides to bless us with physical comforts such as a home of our own or a stable vehicle. However, such luxuries will not bring more joy to my life. My joy flows from the Holy One and the hope that I can impact other people for Him.

For Melinda's birthday in October 2004, I wrote the following poem for her to help us remain joyful for the right reasons.

Woman Of My Dreams

You are the one woman of my dreams,
Making my heart burst at the seams.
I do not deserve your love or care,
But I know you are always there.
Years upon years, forever and a day,
Your tenderness I can't repay.
Although all I have when times are tough,
My words and love hardly seem enough.

Faithful disciple, wife, and now a mother,
More than an aunt for another,
Sacrificing everything for us all
You are heeding the Savior's call.
Stay focused and trust in Him,
Even when the light looks dim.
When the future ahead looks so bleak,
Christ can be strong when we are weak.

When you need a shoulder, look to me,
Together we will pray and see
What God has planned for our years
And permit Him to calm our fears.
Houses, land, and cars are all nice,
But the Lord will remain our life's spice.
Love is the key to a joyous life,
Making me proud you are my wife!

Chapter 10:
Bringing It All Together

A Life Built On Faith

The success that God has placed in my life simply amazes me. I often wonder what those doctors, who said I would be better off in an institution, would think if they could see all I have accomplished so far in my life. My life truly makes me joyful, with a wonderful wife, a beautiful daughter, a nephew who is like my own son, and a wonderful Savior who gives me abundant joy. This life of mine became a reality only because of my previous accomplishments made possible by God.

God's plan for my life has been incredible so far. I attended college because of my academic excellence in earlier schooling, which occurred because of my disability. I made many friends in college because I dared to expand my independence by living on campus. I met Melinda as a result of making so many friends.

Now, Melinda and I have a wonderful family. We may not be rich, far from it in fact, but I am truly happy and joyful. Physical comfort does not equate to being happy. True joy comes from the knowledge that Christ saved you and that God is working in your life. We plan on living a long time, so I can't wait to see how else God will bless us in the many years we have ahead of us!

God's greatest gift in my life

Conclusion

The true key to a joyful life rests in the ability to recognize God's fingerprints on different events in your life, whether they are there from creating the moments or just molding them into a tool He can use. The occurrence may seem as trivial as a phone call or as monumental as a marriage, but they all are part of God's master plan for you! When you are able to look into your past and see how God has used experiences in your life to put you exactly where you are now, you can have confidence in the present and future, even in hard times, that God knows what He is doing. That is true joy! True joy frees you from being worried and over-stressed; it frees up your time and energy so you may worship Him who brings joy to your life.

God has used my disability in incredible ways and I know He will continue to use me for His Kingdom. My family and I might not have found Christ if I weren't disabled. With that in mind and the other fantastic blessings in my life, I can honestly say that I would not go back and change my condition even if I could because I have no guarantee that I would be a Christian if I were able-bodied. My physical freedom is a small amount to pay for the spiritual freedom I have in Christ Jesus—a small price to live *a life with purpose!*